Drill Your Way to Great Putting

George Connor

Editor John Torsiello

Photographs by Mark Paul

Table of Contents

Forward

I have known George for over a decade and found him to be a consummate golf professional in every aspect.

From a teaching perspective George continues to educate himself on techniques, communication skills and the overall game of golf. As a professional, George uses the latest in video and analysis with every student to allow him or her to understand their golf swings and see a path to improvement, the latter always foremost in his mind.

Many golf professionals I have encountered over my years in the game come to the lesson tee without video equipment or training aids. They rely on their eyes solely to evaluate a student, demonstrate the swing, and then have students watch their swing to try and have those taking the lesson understand what is being taught. But George has invested in his craft with the latest in video, 3-D analysis, computerized diagnostics and training aids to help his students improve. And the results show. You do not become the Connecticut PGA Section Teacher of the Year twice through luck.

I'm happy to say that George has been a guest instructor in our publication, Golfing Magazine (www.golfingmagazine.com), and readers have found him to be knowledgeable, insightful and easy to understand.

But more than a golf professional, I have known George to be an outstanding individual and family man. He truly cares about giving back to his students, to the game of golf and to society in general. George is leaving a mark on the game, and life, and we are all better for it.

I'm pleased to have been asked to write the forward to his book on putting drills. George has invested countless hours in this book for one reason; to make anyone who reads it a better putter. Any golfer who practices the many drills George has detailed will most likely become a much improved putter of the ball, and therefore see his or her score become lower.

There is no one aspect of the game that is more vital to scoring well than putting. For the average player, almost half the shots taken during a round will come on the putting green. As George says in this book, too few golfers practice the art of putting, instead heading to the driving range to pound drivers in an endless quest for more distance.

Take advantage of the wisdom George has imparted to us in this book and I'm sure you will be walking off the course with lower scores and feeling a whole lot better about your game.

Tom Landers

Publisher, Golfing Magazine

Preface

Congratulations on having the interest to read this book. What follows is a compilation of drills you can use to enhance your skills in all the key aspects of putting. Before deciding which of the drills you will use, a little analysis would be a great place to start. Analyzing where your strengths and weaknesses lie will allow you to most productively use your practice time. It is easy and fun in the short term to "practice" what you are good at. In the long term however, this approach will not go very far toward improving your overall putting performance. Included in this text are drills to make your stroke more repeatable, your distance more precise. Then there are drills to teach you to handle the pressure that you may face in competition. Based on where you are in the realm of putting skills, choose drills that will help you reach your goals.

Once you have a list of drills in place, it is time to get to work. The key to any improvement plan is consistency. I tell all my students that we should approach learning or improving golf skills the way we should have approached school work. When I was in school, I would have had much more success and a stress free, higher GPA if I had spent a regular dose of studying rather than pulling all night study marathons at the 11th hour. So, your putting practice plan should be made up of many short sessions as opposed to a few long sessions done sporadically.

Depending on the drills you are doing, within 20 to 30 minutes you can complete as many as five different drills. Other drills will take longer so you may only do one or two drills during a given session. Keep your putting sessions to 30 minutes or less. Trying to practice continuously for an hour or more will lead to thoughtless, distracted practice, which will end up causing more harm than good. Set aside a bit of time four or five times per week. During the off-season, these sessions may be five to 10 minutes in your living room. During the season, you will want to lengthen the sessions, and the fun drills will make the sessions enjoyable as you improve.

Over the course of a year, you will want to change your practice drills often. You will be doing this for two reasons.

- You want to keep your practice routine fun. If you do the same drills for too many weeks in a row you can easily become bored and your sessions will lack the attention they deserve
- As you move through practice sessions your skills will change. When you start out, there may be one or two glaring deficiencies that need immediate attention. Once those are improved significantly you will want to address the other areas as well.

How good do you want to be? The answer to that question will help you decide how much practice time is suitable and what drills will best allow you to reach goals.

A Suggested Time Allotment for Putting Practice Based on Skill Level Desired

How Good You Want to Be	Total Practice Time Per Week (in hours)	Number of Practice Sessions Per Week
Professional	10	20*
Collegiate Player	8	16*
0-8 Handicap	3	6
9-15 Handicap	2	6
16+	2	8

*20 or 24 sessions per week? Yes. Keeping each putting session to 30 minutes maximum, you will complete multiple session each of your six days of practice per week. At the end of any putting session, go and do something else (lunch, chipping, full-swing, play nine holes, etc.) for at least 30 minutes before returning to the putting green.

Chapter 1
Who I Am and Why I Wrote This Book

I have been teaching golfers for almost 20 years in and around New England. I have been named at different times by Golf Digest and Golf Magazine as one of the best instructors in my area. On two occasions, the Connecticut Section of the PGA of America named me Teacher of the Year. Over that time I have been fortunate to introduce the game to golfers, helped many players win tournaments, attain college scholarships, and launch professional careers. I have always had a passion for helping people become better putters. I see putting as an opportunity for anyone to become "great." In all honesty, there are many people that play golf who will never drive the ball long distances, or have the strength and speed to hit towering iron shots that hit the green and stop. When it comes to putting anyone can become great and 95 percent of the people playing golf can reduce their scores and their frustration level by putting better. Taking this one step further; if you are a poor putter there will be limited rewards for improving in the other areas of the game. If you have virtually no chance of holing putts from five to 12 feet as an example, what is the benefit of hitting difficult bunker shots close or knocking a long iron to 10 feet for birdie?

As I became more and more involved in teaching people to putt better, I came to the realization that putting appears to be easy but at the same time mysterious. It seems too easy to take a lesson about how to putt better and too mysterious to know what to do to improve. As a result, poor putters go through their golf careers, neglecting putting skills and living with the frustration and wasted shots that their weak skills cause. Nationally, only 6 percent of golf instruction centers on putting. When we consider that more than 40 percent of the strokes during an average round are taken with the putter, the math seems ludicrous.

I have achieved certification from three superb institutions. If you are not familiar with these three companies I would encourage you to do a little bit of research.

- Aimpoint Technologies: As stated below, accurately predicting how much a putt is going to curve as it rolls to the hole is a core skill required to make more putts. For as long as golf has been played, green reading remained somewhat a mystery. There are countless myths and lore surrounding why putts break a certain way at certain geographic areas. Founder Mark Sweeney created Aimpoint Technologies and removed all the guesswork and mystery from this important aspect to putting. There are two different ways we teach people the science of reading greens.

The introductory system, "Express," is incredibly easy to learn and does a wonderful job of identifying where you should aim. The traditional method is a bit more complex but also 100 percent accurate. I have been a Certified Aimpoint Instructor for a number of years and it gives me both the ability to travel to some wonderful clubs and more importantly to offer golfers the total formula for great putting. Aimpointgolf.com

- SeeMore Putter: Since Payne Stewart won the US Open at Pinehurst using the unusual looking SeeMore FGP putter, these wands have been used by great putters. The company now offers a complete line of putters with any head design you could desire. Beyond their innovation and high quality what separates SeeMore putters from others is their Rifle Scope Technology. A simple Red Dot and two white lines will help you gain consistency in your aim and set-up. While there are a lot of great putters on the market, I can't find a reason to putt with anything but a SeeMore. I am a member of the SeeMore Putting Institute (SPi) and enjoy working with all the folks based in Tennessee. SeeMore.com

- EyeLine Golf: Owner Sam Froggatte and his family have grown this training aid business over the years. Sam is always full of energy and, like me, has a passion for helping people putt better. While they offer an assortment of training aids for all parts of the game the company also has many great putting training aids, some of which were developed by others and brought to market by Sam, others he developed himself. The nice thing is Sam doesn't carry just any training aid, each of them are vetted by Sam himself, are helpful , and feature and quality construction. I went through his 4 Elements, which is heavy on practice rather than attempting to pigeon hole a golfer into a specific "method" of putting. Eyelinegolf.com

What I Like to See in a Putting Stroke

I am in no way what is called a method teacher. When it comes to putting, I see all sorts of putters, grips, postures and styles. There may be great putters that look different but in order to be great they all have the ability to do four things very well. Great putters:

- Roll the ball on the line they choose
- Roll the ball the appropriate distance or speed
- Read greens accurately
- Perform the above skills under pressure

My teaching focuses on developing these skills in all golfers. What it takes for one individual to gain these skills will be unique. In other words, not all set-ups and strokes need to look the same. We are striving for the ability to perform consistently on the greens and I am apt to leave (or add) individual traits that will help a golfer become proficient.

That being said, I have some preferences. I always tell students is, if you are doing something well, don't change just because someone else does it differently. But if you are struggling one of the following four areas may be worth some thought. Generally, I like to see:

- <u>A relatively straight mid-back</u>. That is to say that the golfer is not hunched over. Once a golfer puts a lot of curve in his/her back there is a restriction to turning the shoulders, which for many is the engine they are trying to use to move the club.
- <u>Eyes are positioned slightly inside the ball at address</u>. Despite the old saying that eyes must be over the line of the putt, there are too many great putters with their eyes inside the ball to give the old saying any credence. Furthermore, getting eyes directly above the target line tends to lead to hunched backs.

Eyes slightly inside the line of the putt and a straight mid-back

- <u>The shape of the stroke will be a natural arc</u>. With a shaft that leans towards the player, the club head will arc slightly to the inside of the target line in the backswing and follow through.
- <u>A "Standard" Grip</u>. While you can use the same grip that you use for hitting full shots, the most common putting grip is the reverse

over-lap. Rather than the pinkie finger of the bottom hand overlapping onto the fingers of the top hand, the index finger of the top hand will lay onto the fingers of the bottom hand. In the last 15 years we have seen a plethora of unconventional grips. From cross-handed, split-handed to claw grips, pencil grips and the like we have seen some pretty creative approaches. I consider these styles trying to mask poor fundamentals. The way I see it, if you are trying to come up with a way to move the putter reliably there is something causing a problem that should probably be repaired rather than bandaged.

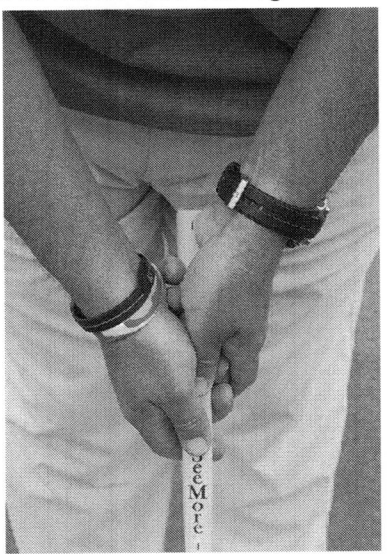

- <u>Keep the putt out of the "life lines" of the hands</u>. For as long as I can remember it has been taught that the putter grip should be placed in the life lines of the hands. Having the putter handle run through the palm of the hands makes it very easy for the wrists to become active during the stroke, which generally is something we try to avoid. I prefer that the heel pad of the top hand (left hand for a right handed player) be at least on the corner of the grip or touching the flat portion on the top of the putter handle. See

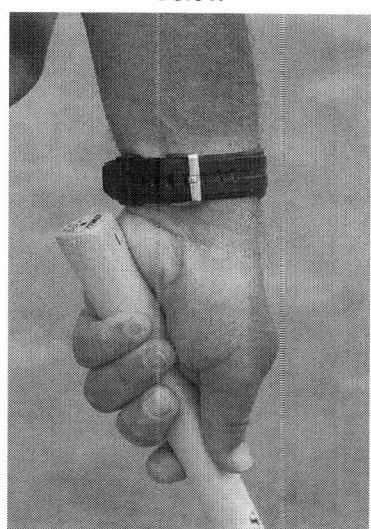

Okay, why did I write this book? In many ways I have been writing it for 20-plus years. Over the course of teaching, I have used drills as a form of testing a skill, teaching a motion or having a player engrain a particular aspect. So, once I started writing them all down in a central place, I realized I had a pretty large document. Now you have one place to look in order to develop extremely effective and fun practice routines.

When practicing any aspect of golf, I encourage you to remember three important aspects must be present:

1. There must be accurate feedback during practice. In the full swing this might be as simple as the ball flying a certain way. Ideally there is some tangible measure of what the club is doing or what the body is doing during the swing. In the short game, and especially when putting, the feedback within the drills can be anything from did the ball roll on line? How far did it travel? Did it go in the hole?
2. Practice sessions must be fun and engaging. They must keep your attention if they are going to be productive. Using games and

drills are the perfect way to do this. Because you will be repeating the same drills on different occasions you may find this approach has you excited to improve on your best score or performance during a particular drill.

3. You should be more confident after a practice session than you were before it. Remember that parts of each practice session should address your weaknesses. When working on these areas, use drills or parameters that you feel you can achieve. Over time, slowly make the drills harder to match your improving skill set. I don't want anyone to attempt during a practice session what they have no chance of achieving. Make your practice sessions challenging but not impossible. If they are the latter practice is neither fun nor good for your confidence. If you get beat up emotionally doing a particular drill, balance that off with doing another drill that will make you feel better about one of your abilities.

Lastly, there are two general "types" of practice. Block practice is where you perform the same task over and over. This might be hitting the same 10-foot putt a number of times in a row, or rolling balls down a yardstick until you can do it properly 20 times in a row.

Random practice is simply not hitting the same shot twice in a row. You might have a series of putts that you hit in order a few times, as in the Four Points drill, or where you never hit the same putt twice, as in the Gauntlet.

There is a place for each of these forms of practice. The drills in this book are a thoughtful combination of block and random practice. Much of the random practice will be in the form of the games discussed in the last chapter, where there is always a score or a result to strive for or exceed.

Chapter 2
Finding the Right Putter for You

Golf has gotten very high tech hasn't it? We have GPS, or lasers, to measure distance to targets. Anyone buying a new driver can optimize their head type and shaft on a radar machine. Irons are custom fit to the player and wedges are often "gap fitted" using launch monitors. Once it comes to putting, technology gets pushed aside by some. Golfers continue to "guess" how much a putt will break. Golfers buy their putter, the club used more than any other in the bag, based on looks or popularity.

I encourage you to get a putter that is fit to you. A properly fit putter will make you a better putter. We all know there are many types of putters available. Manufacturers have introduced to the market every conceivable shape, color, material, etc. How can you decide what is right for you? It certainly can get confusing! Here are the check points I go through in order to fit someone to a putter:

Head Style: For any golfer there will be head styles (mallet, blade, alignment markings, no markings, rounded back, and straight back, off-set) that will help or hinder your ability to aim the putter accurately. Most golfers will have a bias of aiming either left or right. They don't aim there on purpose. But when their eyes triangulate there is a distortion, and while they think they have the putter aimed perfectly, it actually will be to one side or the other. It is rare for a golfer to misalign the putter in both directions. I see golfers that are always left while others are always right. In a putter fitting, this would be addressed and you may well find that certain characteristics in the style of putter you use will help to neutralize this. There is not a steadfast rule but here is an example: I see that golfers who aim left are often better with a putter that has a rounded back edge instead of a straight line. Straight shafts, plumber's neck hosels and the like will all act to help or hinder the perception of where you are aiming the putter.

Length: We are not fitting anchored or broom handle putters anymore, but the length of the shaft if proper will encourage you to get into a good posture. Proper posture allows for a lack of tension in your neck, back, shoulders and arms. The length of the putter can also get your eyes into the optimum position.

Lie Angle: The angle at which the shaft comes out of the head is often "tweaked" to promote a variety of aspects, including stroke shape and eye position relative to the line of the putt. Because there is loft on a putter, if the lie angle is wrong, the face will actually be facing left or right of target even when the leading edge of the putter is perpendicular to the line. I often use lie angle adjustments along with shaft length to get a student into a posture in which they will perform best.

Loft: Yes, a putter has loft. The standard, off the rack putters will have anywhere from two to four degrees of loft. A putter will need to be looked at based on an individual's putting stroke and the loft is often changed a bit. Matching loft to the stroke can help promote the ball roll smoothly at the beginning of its journey.

Head Weight: It is common for a putter head to weigh anywhere from 320 to 360 grams. Moving through weight from one end of the range to the other can often help a player develop good distance control. If you typically play on fast greens, you will want to have a putter on the heavier end of the scale. A lighter putter will be a benefit if your home course has slow greens. When I say this to students the relationship of weight to green speed seems wrong. Please keep in mind that the head weight can help you control the speed that it travels through impact. On fast greens you don't want it moving too fast so the added weight will help. Whereas on slow greens, a lighter head will move naturally faster and transfer more energy into the ball.

Handle Size: There are a few ways to help players control unwanted motion in their wrists during a putting stroke. While I prefer to accomplish this with the way the hands are positioned on the club, it is not uncommon to increase the size of the grip to help the wrists and hands remain neutral during the stroke.

You are going to use your putter more than any other club in your bag. Please take the time to get a putter fit to you. It will help you make more putts and enjoy the game more.

Chapter 3
Building a Reliable Stroke

An interesting phenomenon occurs when I talk to many teaching professionals. While they may be very particular about positions and motions in the full-swing, when it comes to putting they avoid talking about mechanics and say that the "stroke doesn't matter." If only that were true! Having a consistent and reliable stroke is one of the cornerstones to great putting. There is no need to copy anyone else's style. But any great golfer has developed a stroke that has evolved into a reliable motion that starts the ball on the correct line, with the right amount of energy.

Set-Up Station

Consistency of set-up is a key to building a reliable and repeatable putting stroke. If the ball position, eye position, distance from the ball, posture and stance width are going to be ever so slightly different each time you hit a putt, your stroke will be forced to accommodate these minute changes.

If you have a practice area at home, this can be a permanent set-up. If you are bringing it outside, you will do best to have a few measuring devices and props.

We will want to assure that each time our starting position is the same, so we will need a ruler to measure stance width and distance from the ball. Measure your stance width from inside the heels. Measure your distance from the ball from the toe box of your shoes. Taking two alignment sticks and mark three spots on one of the sticks. The three marks will be for your stance width (2) and one for your ball position. Lay one stick just behind your heels and the other stick will be placed perpendicular to and will point to where the ball position should be. I ike to use a towel when I am outside for this. If you are going to be standing in one spot on the putting green for any significant time, it is a good idea to stand on a towel anyways. (Too long in one spot will end up leaving ghastly dead footprints on the green, so a towel will make the greenskeeper happy!) You can mark where your feet should be, where the ball should be and so on. A mirror is a great aid here to check that your eye position and shoulder alignment is the same each time you roll the ball.

Lastly, you will want to assure that the putter face is aligned properly. Indoors, this can be a line on the carpet or better yet a yardstick that points towards your target. Outside, you can use a tee to lightly scrape the grass where the leading edge of the putter should be.

Turn Don't Tilt

Here is a great drill designed to give you the feel of your shoulders and upper back being the engine of the putting stroke. There is a fundamental difference between shoulders turning versus tilting. What I like to see from the shoulders in the putting stroke is a rotation of the shoulders.

With your putting grip, stand erect, holding the putter out in front of you so that the putter is horizontal to the ground at waist height. From here, make some "strokes," moving the putter on the horizontal plane.

Next, lower your posture so that the putter is now below horizontal but not yet where the putter is soled on the ground. Keep your posture upright enough that the putter head is still 18 inches or so above the ground. Make some strokes from this position. On this plane you will again feel the shoulders as the engine of the stroke and see clearly the arc that the putter naturally swings along.

Coin Drill

Here is a great drill to build a smooth stroke. A stroke without jerky movements is a vital foundation to developing a keen ability to roll the ball the correct speed. The only requirement is that you have a putter with a large enough flat surface to rest a small coin on the putter.

With the coin in place, make a series of practice strokes, feeling the length of a stroke required to hit putts anywhere from 10 to 15 feet. The coin should stay on the flange of the putter at least until you get well into the follow through. If, however, your stroke has a jerky, uneven or sudden transition from back swing to forward swing, the coin will slide off the flange. After getting into a smooth groove with practice swings, start hitting putts from different distances, keeping the coin on the putter at least until after impact.

No Thumbs

For golfers that are either too mechanical or try to steer the putter through the stroke, this is a great drill to give the player a feeling of the putter swinging during the stroke. You will find that a swinging putter is much more consistent than a putter being moved manually through the stroke. This drill also gives the player a feeling of the grip supporting its underside and removing pressure from the front of the grip, where it quite frankly doesn't belong.

With your normal set-up, keep everything the same except to leave your thumbs off the putter. Start with some practice strokes and then hit some medium length putts (five to 15 feet).

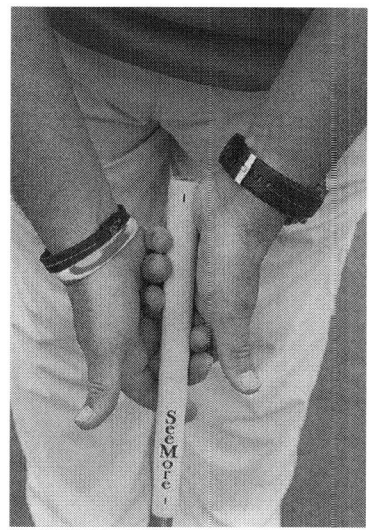

Many instructors have their students hit putts with only one hand to try and achieve the same free swinging putter. While this isn't a bad idea, I find that in order to get the stroke started with one hand the golfer actually gets that one hand more involved than ever.

Stroke Ratio Drill

Too many golfers have a ratio in the stroke that I would describe as 30/70 or 20/80. By this I mean the distance the putter head travels from the start of the forward swing to the end of the follow through could be measured as 30 percent before impact and 70 percent after impacts. This short a backswing and long finish opens the door to both line problems and distance control issues.

Build a barrier that will give you feed back about how long the follow through is. You can use a yardstick resting on the top of shoe boxes, an alignment stick on some head covers, pretty much anything will work. Make some practice strokes to judge how long of a backswing you would typically make for the particular putt. Noticing how long your backswing is, position the ball relative to the barrier so that the follow through can be no longer than the backswing. As you strike putts, you will feel that you are translating a consistent amount of energy to the ball. Some golfers will need to adjust to a longer backswing than they would normally take.. This is to be expected.

Ball in Wrist

Here is a great drill to check and/or eliminate excessive wrist action during the putting stroke. In most cases, any wrist flipping during the stroke is to be avoided. This added hinge will cause both speed and direction problems.

Once you have taken your normal putting grip, place either a golf ball or a tennis ball between the grip and your trailing wrist. The ball should be held against the grip by the inside of your wrist, exactly where you would take your pulse.

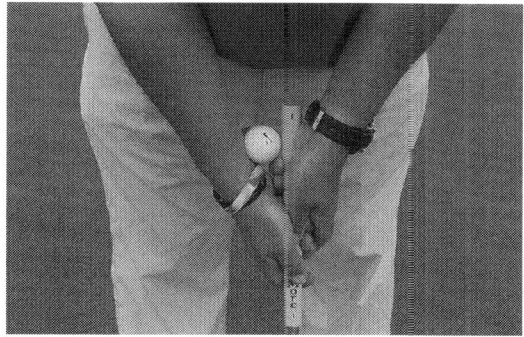

Now, make some practice strokes without the ball dislodging. Once you get accustomed to this start hitting putts of varying lengths, all the while leaving the ball undisturbed between your trail wrist and the handle of the putter.

*If you find this too difficult you most likely have not created enough forward motion of the putter and as such, need the flipping of the wrists to create the motion. If this is the case, use the **Torso Rotation Drill, Thumbs Off** and the **Putting Rod Drill** to engage more shoulders as the engine of the stroke.*

Sweet Spot

This drill is as much a test as it is a skill builder. Feedback is important when you are practicing and this simple drill won't fail in that regard.

Striking the ball on the same spot of the putter face time and time again is a huge factor in starting the ball on line and at the right speed. The smaller any dispersion, the more precise you will be in the above skills. Hitting the ball with different parts of the face will cause different "impact ratios," which is a fancy way of saying that all other things being equal, the ball will travel different distances.

There are two ways to set-up this drill. You can use toothpicks and clear cellophane tape, or pick up some SweetSpot 360's from Eyeline Golf. Either way, we want to frame the sweet spot of the putter.

You will need two toothpicks. Break them in half. Now use the four pieces to build a box around the sweet spot and run one or two pieces of tape over the face to hold them in place. I like to leave these on for a few days or a week while I do my other drills.

Putter Gate

This is another way to check that you are hitting the sweet spot and also relates to the path of the putter as well.

Find a nice straight putt on the practice green, anywhere from six to 10 feet. Place your putter at address so that the sweet spot is exactly where it should be at impact. Now place one tee just outside the toe of the putter and one just inside the heel. If you are inside, you can turn the tees upside down and place them on the floor. Start to hit putts. If the ball is coming off the right spot on the putter, both tees will be undisturbed.

The Pen Is Mightier

Refuting the idea of trying to keep the putter low to the ground in the backswing, this drill will help you maintain a constant radius during the stroke.

Take a pen and place it 10 inches behind the ball, perpendicular to the target line. As you are making strokes, the putter head should be in the air high enough to clear the pen.

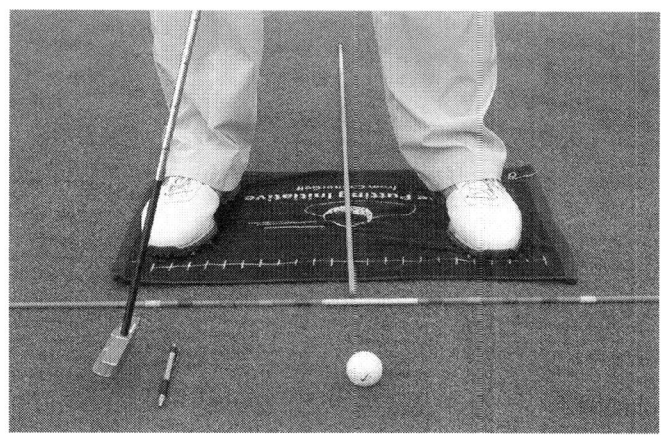

In regards to the putter staying low or not in the backswing, think about what will have to happen for the putter to move away from the ball 12, 18 inches or more and stay low to the ground. For this to happen, either the arms would in a sense need to get longer (elbows extending), or your center (think mid-back) would have to move away from the target. Neither of these movements are desirable in creating a simple, repeatable motion.

Pre-made Training Aids

Putting Arc

Because the putter head will move into the air in the back swing and follow through, it is natural for the heel of the putter to work slightly inside and away from the target line in the backswing and the follow through. There are a few rails available on the market that will give you the feeling of the putter being on the proper plane through the swing. Of those available, I like the Edge Putting Rail from EyeLine Golf. It is available in different angles, 70 degrees being the most common. It is also made of metal, so you get the feel and auditory feedback of the putter dragging on the metal rail throughout the stroke.

Putting Sticks

This is to help you find and develop a consistent radius. It is a simple device that on one end rests on the flange of the putter and the other wedged just under the sternum. While making a stroke the rod should stay connected to you and the putter. Any change in the radius will cause the rod to disconnect from the body. These are available from EyeLine Golf as the Pendulum Putting Rod or from Golf Around the World as the Matchstick.

Triangulator

Here is another "low tech" but very helpful device to have in your putting toolbox. From the SeeMore Putter Company, the Triangulator is a great way to check your alignment. Place the raised edge of the triangle against the face of your putter. Anchor the triangle and then run the string to the target. There are grooves in the triangle to assure that the string is going in the exact angle.

I also like to use the Triangulator when I set up a putting station. Take time to make sure it is perfect and then lightly scratch the grass with a tee along the raised edge of the triangle. This will place a line on the green so you know that your putter face is square. Shown below.

Balls of Steel

This is another helpful aid from EyeLine Golf. These are "golf balls" that are five times the weight of a normal ball. I use these with students to work on the ratio of the stroke, sweet spot contact, and to encourage the golfer to get some "life" in their stroke. Extremely slow and diligent strokes may make sense but remember it is still about transferring energy to the ball.

Chapter 4
Starting the Ball on Line

Starting the ball on the exact line you have chosen is one of the core skills in putting. Golfers tend to take it for granted but it is rare to find a player that can start the ball on line time and time again. Furthermore, if you assembled a group of 50 golfers that could roll the ball on line on a straight putt, less than half of them would be able to do it on a breaking putt.

Where the ball starts is almost exclusively determined by where the face of the putter is aligned at impact. The path that the club takes has some effect. But the putter face is responsible for more than 90 percent of the starting direction of a putt. Therefore, if we can deliver the face of the putter in the desired orientation at impact we have taken a big step towards making a lot of putts.

There is a bit of an anomaly when it comes to the importance of putting skills. In the next chapter I talk about proper speed, which may change your thinking. When it comes to hitting the ball on the proper line, many golfers will immediately think about hitting short putts. Perhaps there is a tendency to push or pull the short ones and it is these putts that get you thinking about the importance of the line. There is no doubt that you need to start the ball on line in order to hole a lot of short putts. However, on long putts and mid-range putts starting the ball on line becomes even more crucial to success. If you start a ball one degree off line from nine feet but do everything else perfect the ball can still go in the hole. Outside of 10 feet, a one-degree error is enough to keep the ball from being holed. When we are 20 feet away and have significant break on a putt, a relatively small miss of your starting line can make you look foolish.

A mainstay in your putting tool box is an elevated aim line. We can use two knitting needles and some string with stretch. Having this at your disposal will allow you to move around the putting green and set the line up wherever you like. When I was a kid we used to snap down a chalk line on the green using a carpenter's tool. The problem with this is that the line is there for a number of days and unless you can make lines all over your practice putting green, you are now stuck to that location.

Push Drill

Since the alignment of the putter is the overriding factor that determines the direction of the ball, the Push Drill addresses this aspect specifically. Find a straight, uphill putt. With a ball no more than 18 inches from the hole, take your normal set up position. Without making a backswing, move the putter forward only and with enough speed so that the ball will separate from the putter. If the putter is square, you will see the ball roll into the center of the hole. If the face rotates left or right while in contact with the ball, this will be visible to you.

To shrink your room for error and to make the feedback more clear, you can set up a gate for the ball or use a yardstick, as I talk about below.

Yardstick

This is one of my favorites. It is an indoor drill only, but one that you should be doing all year long on a regular basis.

Pick up a metal yardstick from your local hardware store. Metal works better than wood as it will be smoother. A metal yardstick also will have a small hole drilled into it at one end. Put a golf ball so that it rests in the hole and hit the putt, attempting to keep the ball rolling on the ruler all the way to the end. If the putter does not stay on line it will roll off one side of the yardstick before it reaches the end. If it stays on the yardstick the entire time you have rolled a ball with one degree of being perfectly on line. If your error is less than one degree and all other factors are correct (speed and line) that is good enough to make a ball from 10 feet.

There is an added benefit with this drill. Setting up with your putter square to the end of the yardstick will help train your eyes, so that you know where the putter is aimed.

Elevated Aim Line

There are a few pre-made products you can purchase but you can just as easily make this at home. Using two knitting needles and some round elastic thread you can build an elevated aim line. Simply tie each end of the round elastic thread to a knitting needle and you are ready to go.

When you are outside on the putting green you can stick one of the knitting needles at your target then stretch the string and stick the other knitting needle behind the ball. This will create a aim line that runs above the intended line of your putt.

You can use this drill a few different ways to check that your ball rolls on line. If your eyes are over the ball you will be able to see that the ball rolls on the proper line. If your eyes are inside the line, which I prefer, the optics will not be optimal but you can easily use the line to make a gate for the ball to pass through. Building a gate is nothing more than sticking two tees a few feet in front of the ball. Put on tee on each side of the line. You can be kind to yourself and give yourself a little bit of extra space. But as you get better you should shrink the gate so that only a near perfect put will fit through it. *See Ball Gate Drill below*.

Ball Gate

As described above, a ball gate is nothing more than obstacles that the ball will travel through if it is on line. You can do this indoors or out with nothing more than two tees. When outside, you can stick them in the ground, indoors, flip them over and stand them up.

Where you put the gate depends on the type of putt you are working on. If it is a straight putt you can build the gate a few feet in front of the ball. If it is a breaking putt however, you will want to place the gate within 10 inches of the ball. If slope is present the ball will start to break almost instantly, so you do not want to have the gate too far out in front of the ball.

This is a particularly good drill to do on breaking putts. Combined with an Elevated Aim Line, the gate will give you the feedback of where you actually start your putts. Many golfers can roll the ball on the proper line if the putt is straight. Fewer will be able to start the ball on their intended line if break is introduced, so be sure to use this on both left to right and right to left breaking putts.

Two Balls

A ball that leaves the putter rolling down the intended line will be mostly due to where the putter face is aligned at impact. The putter face has more than a 90 percent influence on where the ball starts. This drill will give you the feedback of your tendency.

Find a perfectly straight 10 foot putt, or if indoors, a flat area. Place two balls side by side and perpendicular to the target line. Make sure there is at least a ½ inch between the two balls. Now hit both balls at the same time. A square putter face will cause the balls to roll side by side, with neither ball crossing into the path of the other.

Do not worry if one ball rolls faster or further than the other. You are not hitting either ball on the sweet spot so the impact ratios or energy transferred to the balls will vary.

Lip Balm

This is similar to the Two Balls drill. Take a tube of lip balm and place it on the ground perpendicular to the target line.

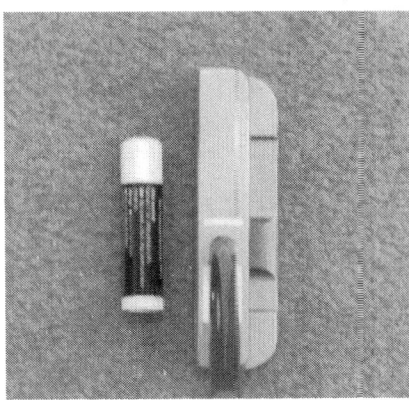

A square putter face at impact will cause the lip balm to roll towards the target. If the putter face is not square however, the putter will not strike the tube flush and it will spin.

Feel free to substitute almost any cylinder for this drill, such as a short piece of PVC pipe.

S-L-S-R

As I mentioned when talking about the elevated aim lines, honing your ability to start the ball on line when faced with a breaking putt is often more of a challenge. Since almost every putt outside of four feet will have some break, this is a skill every great putter must have.

Ideally you will have three elevated aim lines for this drill but one or two is fine. Find a straight six to 10 foot uphill putt and place an elevated aim line above the line of that putt. You will want to establish the second and third stations. From the position of the straight ball take two or three small steps in an arc to the right of the straight ball and do the same to the left of the straight ball. These side positions will no longer be straight putts as you will be rolling the ball on an angle across the slope. When you put up your elevated aim lines, the post, stick or knitting needle near the hole will no longer be directly behind the hole but rather off to the side an appropriate distance. This will be your aiming target to allow the ball slope and gravity to curve the ball into the hole.

Straight-Left-Straight-Right Drill

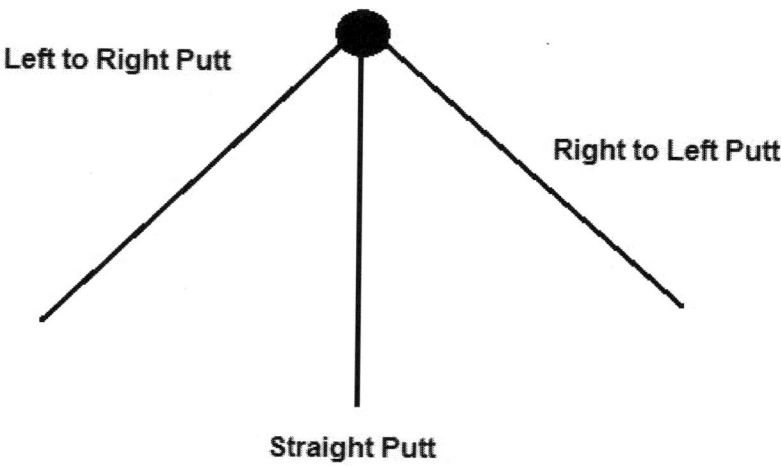

Left to Right Putt

Right to Left Putt

Straight Putt

After hitting 15 or 20 putts straight up the hill, you now want to test your ability to start the ball on line with breaking putts. Start hitting some combination of straight and breaking putts. After a short amount of time working on this drill, I find it best to avoid hitting multiple breaking putts in succession. Keep moving back and forth from the straight putt to a breaking putt. As I refer to the drill as S-L-S-R, hit a straight putt, a left to right, back to the straight and then a right to left.

If you want to make this drill more difficult, you can increase the amount of break for the side putts by increasing the distance you move from the straight putt. As the side putts get closer to travelling perpendicular to the direction of the straight putt, you will be approaching the maximum amount of break for that slope and green speed. You can also set up your stations to create downhill straight, left breaking and right breaking putts.

You may notice that you are particularly less skilled for one direction of break as compared to the other.

Chapter 5
Rolling the Ball the Correct Speed

I truly enjoy talking to people about rolling the ball at different speeds and how important it is to possess the skill to roll it the right distance. For a high handicapper or someone that often three putts, speed is a big problem. Generally speaking, a 30 foot putt will lead to a three-putt, not because you miss the hole four or five feet to right or left but more often because the ball travelled four or five feet too short or too far. Developing the ability to roll the ball at a better speed will allow you to cozy the ball up to the hole for a stress free second putt. Developing the ability to roll the ball the proper speed can reduce a lot of frustration. A few good shots that get you on the green and taking three or even four putts to get the ball in the hole will negate any positive feelings from a good shot.

Lower handicap players often have a window of opportunity to make more putts by fine tuning their ability to roll the ball the proper speed. "Decent" putters will often hit makeable putts that look good as they are rolling but just miss. In most cases the player will blame the amount of break they played. "It doesn't break that much," or "Wow, that really snapped," are common phrases after a putt doesn't break the way the golfer predicted. Sure, a lot of times it is the read that was wrong. But a proper read that assigns an amount of break is directly tied to the speed that the ball will travel.

Regardless of where you fit in the above categories, I want you to take a few minutes to think about how speed impacts the behavior of a putt. As a golf ball rolls along a slope, gravity will cause the ball to turn towards the downhill side of the slope. How much a ball curves is a function of:

- The severity of the slope
- The angle that the ball is rolling relative to the direction of that slope.
- The amount of time the ball is rolling at an angle to that slope

The severity of the slope and the angle that the ball will travel must be determined for any putt. However, the amount of time that the ball will spend rolling from the time it leaves the putter until it reaches the hole will vary and is in large part within the control of the player. Hit two putts from the same spot. Have the first putt go 30 to 36 inches past the hole. Next, hit the second putt so that it just barely reaches the hole. When you do this, set up a gate for the ball to travel through and hit as many putts as it takes until you get one of each speed. What happened? You will notice that both balls broke the same amount but took different amounts of time to do so. The ball that went three feet past may have broken behind the hole while the one that barely reached broke and went in the hole. What we learn from this exercise is that the slope will cause the ball to curve a set amount of distance. Your job as the golfer is to match the amount of break you play with the amount of time the ball will travel until it reaches the hole.

Another exercise is to find a 10 foot putt that will curve quite a bit. Hit a few putts at different speeds and try to see how little break you can play by hitting the putt with a lot of speed and how much break you can play by hitting the ball softer. This will show you that adding time (reducing speed) requires more break and reducing time (adding speed) will require you play less break.

One last point before we get to the drills. There is an ideal speed for a ball to be travelling when it gets to the hole. The less you try to modify that speed from one putt to the next the better off you will be. We have all gotten advice from a playing partner to "hit it firm and take the break out," and we have all tried to die the ball into the hole on other occasions when we were afraid of the ball taking some down hill slope beyond the hole. When we change speeds it becomes difficult to adjust the read or amount of break that is tied to that adjusted speed.

The ideal speed for a ball to travel is where the ball would travel 12 inches past the hole if it didn't hit the hole. Why 12 inches? This is a combination of keeping the hole effectively as big as possible while keeping the ball moving fast enough to not be affected by slight imperfections just in front of the hole. The further past the hole a ball would travel will cause the ball to spend less time over the opening because gravity now has less time to draw the ball down into the hole. Thus, the faster the ball is travelling the closer to the center of the hole the ball must be in order to avoid the ball hitting the edge of the hole but not fall in. "Hit it firm and take the break out" does not take all of the break out and reduces the effective size of the hole.

Three Drills for Better Speed Control

The following three drills represent a good series to do on a regular basis in order to develop or maintain proper speed control. Done in succession they are also a quick way for you to get comfortable with that day's green speed before you go out to play.

Goldilocks

We all remember the story of Goldilocks and the Three Bears. "This one is too hot, this one is too cold," etc. Pick a hole anywhere from 10 to 20 feet away. Then intentionally hit a putt too far, then intentionally hot one too short and then hit the third putt the right distance. This is a simple drill but it will wake up your senses and show you how fast or slow the greens are that day.

Announce

The target for this drill is a line perpendicular to the line of play, not a hole. The line can be a string, an imaginary line between two tees, golf balls, etc.

This is another simple drill where from different distances anywhere between 10 and 30 feet you hit putts with the intention being to stop the ball on the line. For this drill I want you to announce, predict out loud if the ball will stop on the line, short of the line or beyond the line. Announce immediately after the ball is struck and before you look up to watch the ball rolling. You want to announce your gut reaction to the length the putt will travel.

This drill will help you match perception to reality. As an added bonus, it is a quick way for you to get a sense of the green speed that day. If you hit a putt and announce that it will be long, then look up and see that it comes up three feet short of the hole, you will get a shock to your system and awaken your senses to the green speed you will face on the course.

Look at the Hole

From anywhere 10 to 20 feet away from a hole, or strings as described below in the **In the Box** drill, hit putts while looking at the hole. Go through your normal routine but before you start the stroke, look at the target and make your stroke while looking at the target rather than the ball.

This drill taps in to your natural ability to adjust the length of the backswing in order to determine how much energy will go into the ball. I equate it to tossing balls underhand to different targets. If you were to toss bean bags to targets 10, 15 and 25 feet you would adjust subconsciously how far back to swing your arm to hit the target. When you look at the hole while putting, the length of the backswing will often change in length to fit the length of the putt.

Always Shorter

In an effort to improve our feel for hitting putts the right distance, here is a drill where each putt is intended to be a slightly different distance than the putt before it.

From the middle of the practice putting green hit a putt towards the edge of the putting green. The ball should stop on the putting surface and ideally be at least 20 feet. Each successive putt will be hit on the same line and must stop shorter than the one before it   The scoring system here is the how many putts can you hit that stop short of the one before. I like to establish a minimum distance that the ball must travel. So, if the first putt if about 30 feet, how many putts can you hit that travel a shorter distance than the one before it and still travel at least five feet.

The best way to do this would be to leave each putt well short of the one before it. This also quickly causes you to run out of room to hit a lot of putts. As you get better, each putt can be six inches or a foot shorter than the one before it and you will have the ability to hit a lot of putts!

In the Box

Rather than rolling the ball towards a hole, I prefer that you do this drill without a hole, as you can easily get distracted by whether the ball goes in or not. This drill is intended to focus solely on speed.

Take two lengths of string anywhere from three to four feet in length. Lay them on the green perpendicular to the line of play and two feet away from each other. You now have a zone that is two feet deep that you will rolls balls into. From different distances roll balls in an attempt to have the ball stop between the two strings. As it gets easier, shrink the space in between the two strings until you can comfortably roll balls from different distances into a 1 foot area.

In the Box Drill

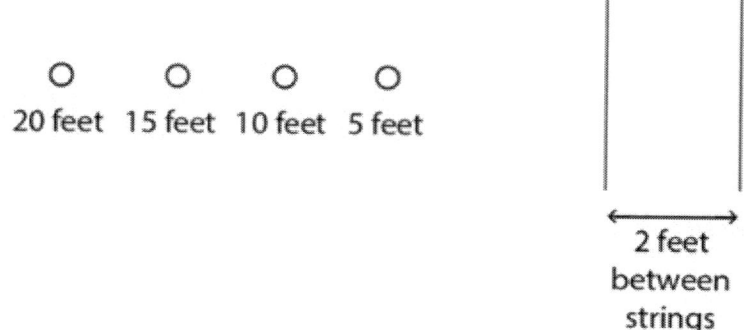

20 feet 15 feet 10 feet 5 feet

2 feet
between
strings

A good routine with this drill is to not hit the same putt twice. Hit one putt each from five, 10, 15 and 20 feet. Do some sets on uphill putts and others on downhill putts. Keep track of how many of the putts are successful so that over time you can see your level of improvement.

You can use this same drill for long putts as well. Make the space between the strings a little bigger and roll 30, 40 and 50 foot putts.

6-Foot Drill

This should be a mainstay in any practice arsenal. The Six-Foot Drill addresses your ability to roll a ball at a precise speed on your "makeable" putts. As I mentioned earlier, expert speed control is a significant factor in making putts. This drill will help you make more of those important 6 to 12 footers.

Here again we will not use a hole. Because we are going to be evaluating the speed of the putt, we do not want a hole to interrupt the rolling ball. Using tees, coins or some string, make a box that is 18-by-18-inches. I like to use an old hole, put down a ghost hole or use a coin in the front side of the box to show where the hole would be.

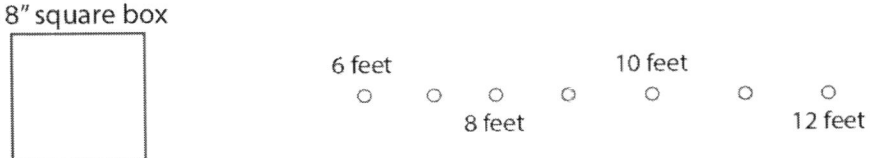

6 foot drill

All the putts need to finish in this box. Start from six feet away. Roll three putts from six feet. If all three balls finish inside the box, stick a tee in the ground at six feet and move back one foot. Hit putts now from seven feet away. If all three putts finish in the box, go to eight feet. As long as every putt finishes in the box keep going back in one-foot increments. However, if any putt comes up short of the box, or rolls through the box and finishes beyond the box, immediately go back to your six-foot starting area and begin again.

Work on this drill for 10 minutes at a time and keep track of how far away from the hole you can get. If you can make all three putts from six to 12 feet, that is 21 putts in a row that are at near perfect speed.

Variations of this drill would be to work on putts that have a decent amount of break, or downhill putts. If it gets easy to do when you start at six feet, start from 10 feet.

Time not Feet

When great putters visualize a putt travelling to the hole, the amount of time the ball will be rolling is part of that visual. The same length putt from different angles will roll very different amounts of time. For example, an uphill 20-foot putt will reach the hole much faster than a 20-foot downhill putt. On "fast greens" a well-paced putt will travel slowly, relative to the faster pace of a similar putt on a slow green. Being able to understand the amount of time a ball will be rolling is a wonderful skill to possess. Having this skill will make it easier for you to understand how much a ball will curve on its way to the hole.

A straight forward way to develop this skill is to simply roll putts for different amounts of time. Find a large open area on the practice green. Roll putts uphill, downhill and across the slope for different amounts of time. Decide how long you want to roll the ball, start counting when you strike the ball and keep counting until the ball stops. Better yet, have a friend with a stopwatch time the ball. (You can find a free stopwatch application for any Smartphone). Roll a ball for four seconds, then six seconds. Notice the difference in distance covered, as well as the difference in the amount of curve as time is added or subtracted. Next, predict how long a ball will be rolling to reach and stop at or just beyond a target. Make a prediction, roll the putt and see how close your prediction was.

When Did It Stop

This drill is best done with a practice partner. It is another way for you to begin to understand how long it will take for a ball to cover a distance given different green speeds and slopes. Roll putts random distances anywhere from 20 to 60 feet. Without looking up or watching the ball, announce when the ball stops rolling.

By having a practice partner working with you, they can watch the ball roll and tell you if you knew exactly when the ball stooped or were a little late in your prediction.

Bull's Eye

This drill is only for long putts. For an above average putter, do this drill from outside of 25 feet. If you are a struggling putter you might want to start this drill from 15 feet. You will hit putts from different distances and gain points based on where the balls finish relative to the hole. You can set up a target with strings, tees or chalk lines or simply measure each putt as you proceed.

Hit 10 putts and keep score. To start off, hit two putts from each distance. Each station will be 10 feet longer than the station before it. Over time, keep the distances that you hit putts from the same and keep track of how your scores improve.

A sample routine for a good putter would be to hit two putts each from 20, 30, 40, 50 and 60 feet.

Let's first establish a point system:

Where did the ball finish	Points
Holed	5 point
Within 2 feet	3 points
Within 3 feet	2 points
Within 4 feet	1 point
Within 5 feet	0 points
Within 6 feet	-1 point
Outside 6 feet	-2 points

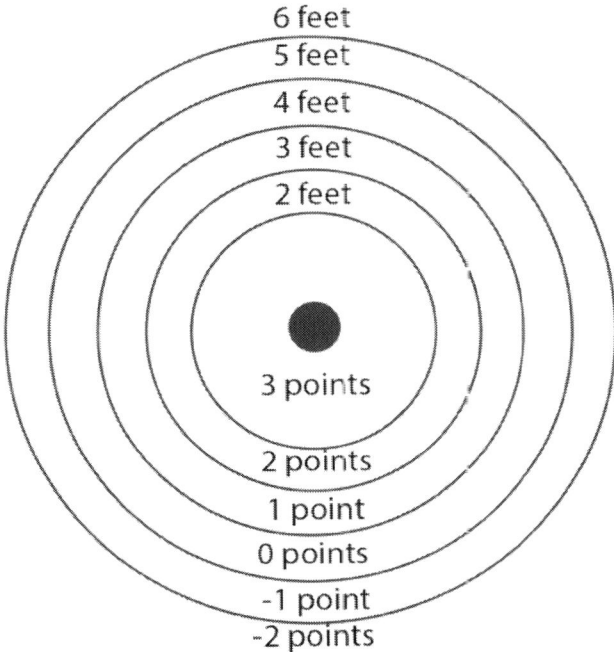

6 feet
5 feet
4 feet
3 feet
2 feet

3 points

2 points

1 point

0 points

-1 point

-2 points

20 Foot Drill

This has long been a staple in my putting drill arsenal. For this drill you will need to be outside on the putting green and you will be putting to a hole. On opposite sides of the hole, pace off 20 feet and stick a tee in the ground or place a coin on the ground. With three balls, start hitting putts with proper speed being the goal.

A successful putt will be either in the hole or in a semi-circle behind the hole. As your skill level increases, you will make the size of the semi-circle smaller. But start off with a half circle the circumference of your putter or three feet, whichever is smaller. The target zone half circle is always on the far side of the hole from where you are putting. The goal is to reach the hole but not go too far past.

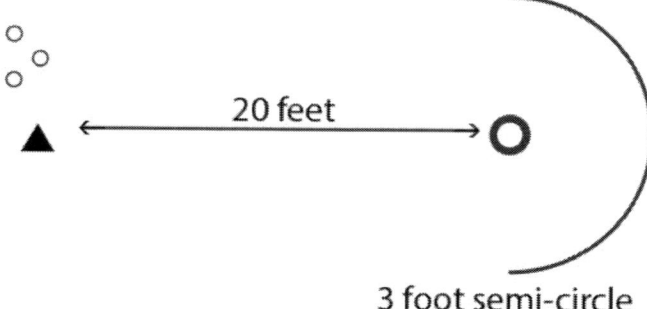

3 foot semi-circle

Start hitting putts from one of the 20-foot markers. If all three putts from that first position are successful, move to the other side of the hole. From that side, start rolling your three putts. If they are all successful, move to the other side. Continue this process as long as you hit putts that either go in the hole or stop in the defined semi-circle. If at any point you hit an unsuccessful putt, you start over.

The goal of the drill is to hit 10 consecutive putts that are successful. For some, this may sound like an easy drill but don't be fooled. You may find it harder to complete than you think. As with the Six-Foot Drill, put a time limit on this. After 15 minutes record the highest number of consecutive putts you hit and make the goal of the next practice session to reach a higher number. If it proves to be too hard, start at 15 feet instead of 20. If it gets easy, make the circumference of the half circle two feet instead of three.

Foot by Foot

Similar to the Ladder Drill we will be putting the ball into a box. For accomplished players, we will be looking to get the ball to finish in a box that is no more than six inches from front to back.

Start at five feet and move back one foot at a time always seeking to have the ball finish in the small area you have defined. Do this on uphill and downhill putts. As you get better, make your first putt from further away. Record how far away from the hole you can get without having a putt come up long or short of the box. As your skill increases over time your speed will be dialed in and you will be sinking more putts.

Chapter 6
Games and Applying Pressure

With the drills that have been described earlier, you have had a chance to isolate particular skills that are required to become a great putter. Having individual skills alone will not, however, allow you to be great if you are unable to perform when it matters. Holing putts on the golf course requires you to be able to apply all your skills at once, sometimes when there may be pressure or you are nervous.

The problem with pressure is, until you have felt it, you don't know how you will react or what you should be doing to perform under stress. Using games on the practice green is a big part of preparing you for the pressure of the course. All of the drills in this section will have a definable score or result. You can use any of these drills first as an assessment. If you find that your score is extremely poor, you may want to re-visit some of the drills listed above to address a particular skill that is preventing you from scoring well.

Keeping a record of your results is a must when undertaking these drills over a period of time. This serves two purposes. First, this will provide you with a tangible indication of your improvement. Secondly, it is a way to put some pressure on yourself. If you know you are approaching your personal best score in one of the games, there will be some added tension. The added tension while doing a drill can help you prepare and deal with the pressure of performing well on the golf course.

Four Points

Almost every golfer that has spent any time practicing his or her putting has done this drill, but it's a good one and can be adapted to fit any skill level. This drill will help you gain confidence on putts inside of five feet. Let's face it, there is no worse feeling than hitting a great shot to four feet and then missing the putt.

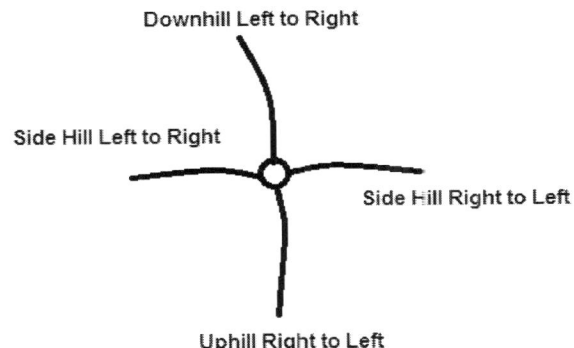

Four Points Drill

The set-up is simple. From four points around a hole hit putts. Think of the points as North, South, East and West on a compass, or 12, 3, 6 and 9 o'clock. In most circumstances this will give you an uphill and downhill putt that is straight or nearly straight as well as a right to left and left to right breaking putt.

You can start off by simply making one putt from each of the four points from three feet away. Then progress to making all four without missing. When that gets easy, make all four from three feet and then four in a row from four feet. When you can make all the putts without missing from three, four and five feet you have holed 12 consecutive putts.

The flatter the slope is around the hole, the easier you are making the drill. Not only beginners need to make it easy, good players that are lacking confidence are well served to spend time making a bunch of short putts with this drill on a relatively flat surface.

To make it more challenging, you can use a hole surrounded by a more severe slope. If you get a little beat up on the harder slope, do one more set on the flatter slope before leaving. I want my golfers to be more confident after a practice session, never less.

The Gauntlet

This is the Four Points drill with more bite and not for the faint of heart. Make 24 consecutive five-foot putts, each from a different spot. That's 24 consecutive putts. Miss one and you start over. You can use different holes but make sure you have an equal mix of uphill and downhill, right and left breakers. It's not easy and you may not complete the drill the first few times you try it, but you will feel bullet proof when you do complete it.

Play Nine Holes

This exercise will act as a predictor of your 18-hole score. Basically, you will play nine holes but each hole will start and finish on the putting green. In random order play three holes from inside of six feet, three holes from seven to 20 feet and three holes from 21 to 40 feet. Do not go in order. I don't want you to start with the shortest putt and work backwards. Mix it up. Play a short hole followed by a long one and then a mid-range as an example. Based on your skill level each putt, or hole, might represent different scores. A world class ball striker might consider a 40 foot putt is for eagle, while short putts may be for par and mid-range putts for birdie. For another player, the short ones may realistically equate to bogey, the mid-range one for par, and long putts represent birdie putts.

Keeping score this way can translates to an 18 hole score and give you an insight into why you are hitting the driver better but your scores haven't changed at all!

Tour Average

This is a mainstay of any putting practice regimen. Test your putting skills against the Tour pros. Based on the statistics of made putts from different distances by PGA Tour pros, you can see where you measure up.

Keep in mind that when you do this drill all putts are on the same line from the hole, or each distance putt is hit from the same spot. You have a great advantage over the Tour pro. You get multiple tries to make the same putt in the drill versus playing golf, where you only have the one chance to make it. For this reason, I ask my better students to use the adaptations to the drill listed below.

Choose a line to the hole and place markers at five, 10, 15 and 20 feet. Then place:

One Ball at Three Feet
Three Balls at 10 Feet
Four Balls at 15 Feet
Five Balls at 20 Feet

3 feet   10 feet   15 feet   20 feet

Tour Average Drill

On each putt, go through the Aimpoint process, then your pre-shot routine and roll the ball. If one putt from each station goes in, you are at the tour average. Using rough averages, Tour Pros make virtually all of their three-footers, 1/3 of their 10-footers, 25 percent from 15 feet and 20 percent from 20 feet.

Adaptation:

To challenge yourself further you can choose a line with more break, or a downhill putt. Pick holes that are on progressive y steeper slopes.

Ultimately, go through the drill with every putt being from a different spot. Example: one five-foot putt will be uphill left to right, the next one down hill right to left. This gives you one chance on each putt and more accurately represents a round of golf.

Make the Must Makes

This is one of my favorite putting drills. It challenges and develops your ability to hole more crucial putts from three to 10 feet. After doing the drill a number of times you will also develop the ability to read more accurate amounts of break within this range and understand how break amounts change as the length of putt is altered. I use this drill a lot with my Aimpoint students. It helps them get used the either using the chart or in making the slight but critical adjustments to break amounts.

Choose a line and place a marker at every foot. You will place six markers on the green. So if your first marker is three feet from the hole you will have markers at three, four, five, six, seven and eight feet from the hole, all on the same line to the hole. This should be done on a consistent slope.

Move from one putt to the next with the goal being to make four of the six putts.

To make the drill the easiest use a small slope on a line that will have a relatively small amount of break.

To make the drill more difficult use steeper slopes and lines where you will need to play more break. You can also hit putts from five to nine feet instead of three to seven.

Add 'Em Up

Hit 10 putts, all on the same line and add up the total distance of made putts. Extending on the same line hit one putt from three, six, nine, 12, 15, 18, 21, 24, 27 and 30 feet. If you make the three- and six-foot putts you are at nine feet total. In order to get to 50 or 60 feet you are going to have to make some long ones.

Over time you will want to see your personal best get a little higher and higher. From one day to the next, vary the putts so that you have small breaks one day and big breaks the next. Some days use uphill putts, other days use downhillers.

Perfect 72

This is an extension of the Four Points Drill. From four points we will hit three putts each from three, six and nine feet. The scoring system is:

- 1 Point for each three-footer you make (12 total points available)
- 2 Points for each six-footer you make (24 total points available)
- 3 Points for each nine-footer you make (36 total points available)

A great score here is 55 points. To make it you will have to hole just about all of the shorter putts and a lot of your nine-footers as well. If you get to that number, or close most of the time, DO NOT hit the same putt twice in a row. In other words, hit one three-footer, one six-footer and one nine-footer from each of the four points and work your way around the hole three times. The scoring is the same but you don't get the opportunity to immediately fix a slightly misread putt.

Chapter 7
Testing Your Skills

We have a limited amount of time to practice. If you are an aspiring competitive player, you need to be working on all facets of your game, not to mention fitness and potentially a hectic travel schedule. If you are a recreational player, you have to balance family and work, so you may find that scratching out 20 minutes here or there is all you can do. Regardless of your situation, it is important that you use your practice time effectively.

In order to assure that you will get the most "bang for your buck" let's make sure you are working first on the areas where there is the most room for improvement. If you test poorly in one area and slightly below average in another, work on the worst first. Once that improves, you can then split your time between continuing to improve in a weak area, while at the same time cleaning up some of the other problem areas.

No matter what skill level you are at, you will want to highlight specific areas of your putting in order to get a clear picture of where you should be spending your practice time. Even some of the best players can not accurately diagnose why some of their putts don't fall. I have heard too many elite players blame their read when speed was the issue. In other cases, a player will unknowingly start the ball well off the intended line.

When I work with a student, I will periodically put them through a complete assessment that will test their ability to aim, start the putt on line, control the speed and hole putts with different amounts of break. At your home course, you can put yourself through an abbreviated version of my assessment. There are a few drills listed in this book that will serve nicely as testing mechanisms. Remember the formula for great putting includes your ability to read the green, start the ball on line, at the correct speed and be able to perform under pressure. This book will not include information on how to read greens. For that I recommend that you get in touch with a Certified Aimpoint Instructor. (You can thank me later.) The other pieces of the formula are included in this book and you should use the following to test your skill levels.

Here is a series of drills taken from the book that you can use to test your skills. Based on your results, you can then tailor your practice routines to work on your weaknesses, while maintaining the areas. If working on your own, this test should be taken once a month so that you always have an accurate understanding of your skills.

Drill/Test	Score	Grade
Yardstick Drill	46+ out of 50	A
	41-45 out of 50	B
	34-40 out of 50	C
	Less than 34	D
Bull's Eye (10 putts)	30+ points	A
	24-29 points	B
	18-24 points	C
	Less than 18 points	D
Perfect 72	60+points	A
	50-59 points	B
	42-49	C
	Less than 42	D

Perhaps the first time you take the test you get a "B" on the Yardstick Drill, a "D" on the Bull's Eye Drill and a "B" on the Perfect 72 Drill. Clearly, in this case your ability to lag long putts close is lacking. You will want to spend more time working on the drills in Chapter 4. Over time you will get better at controlling your speed, so it is now time to turns some of those B's into A's. This is why you will want to re-test regularly.

Printed in Great Britain
by Amazon